FRANCE Activity Journal

From the Author of Learn About France for Kids

What's in This Book

Journal

The book includes 60 daily journal pages. 30 are filled with prompts, and 30 are blank for doing whatever you want (e.g., drawing a picture, taping in a souvenir, or writing more because you have a lot to say).

There are some slight differences in the prompts, so flip through and complete whichever one suits the day you just had. For example, if you laughed a lot on a particular day, fill in the page with the prompt "What made me laugh?". It's okay if the journal pages are out of order; you can even miss days. Or you can complete as many pages as you want on a day full of adventures you don't want to forget. Just put the correct date on the top of the page, and away you go!

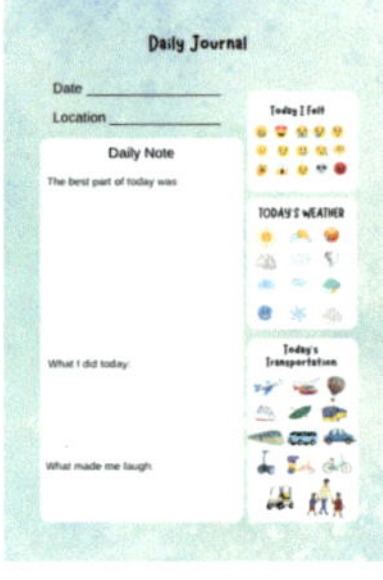

Puzzles, Games and Mazes

There are fun France-themed games throughout the book. They are placed in different spots that make sense for your trip. For example, there's an Airport/Train Station Bingo game at the front of the book and another at the back. These will help you fill the times you must wait around for sometimes hours at a time.

Where a puzzle has a specific answer, like a maze, you'll find these at the back of the book.

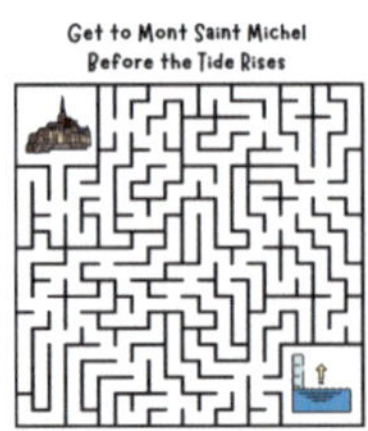

Templates, Tips & Facts

We included some handy tips, like packing your suitcase and carry-on and preventing jet lag. Although an adult is likely to pack for you, it's helpful to understand these tips to be more independent when you travel. Soon, you'll become an experienced globetrotter!

France is a fantastic country, and there is so much to experience. So, we added a few facts throughout the book to help you better understand what you might see.

Bon Voyage en France!

Enjoy your trip to France!

This book belongs to:

Name ___________________ Age_______

I'm going to France!

Date we leave: ______________________________

Date we come home: __________________________

Who's coming with me: _______________________

____

____

How Far Will You Travel?

Can you find your country on this map? Colour it in, then draw an arrow to France (that's the blue country in the middle of the map).

Next, circle how you will get there.

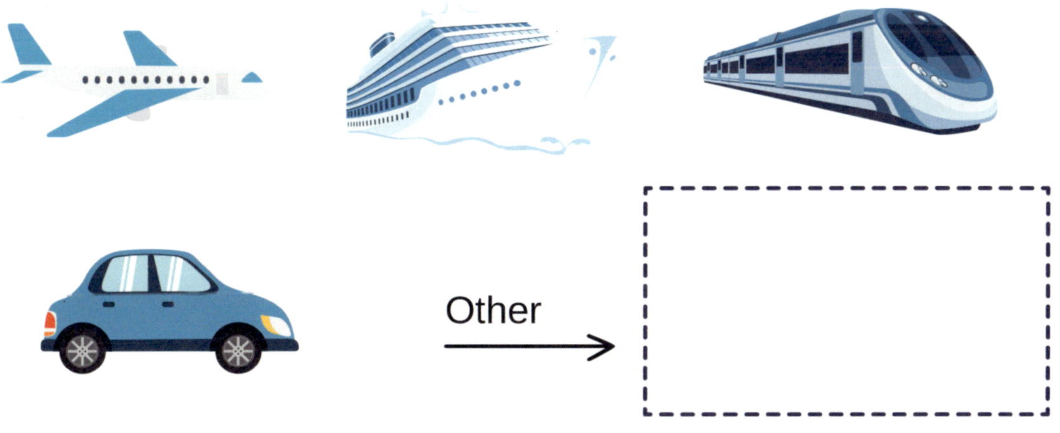

Tips for Packing Your Suitcase For a Flight

1. Keep a packing list.
2. Don't overpack - leave room for souvenirs.
3. Stick to a colour theme for your clothes to mix and match your outfits.
4. Even if where you're going is warm, always pack a sweater or jacket.
5. Pack little things inside of big things. For example, pack some socks inside your hat.
6. Place something outside your suitcase to immediately recognize it on the airport carousel. For example, tie a short ribbon of your favourite colour to the handle.
7. Don't wait until the last minute. Begin packing a few days before you leave with your checklist nearby. As you think of things, add them.
8. Finally, remember to bring some entertainment for downtime at your accommodation. You may not have English TV to keep you occupied, so activity books or small pocket games are a good idea.

Suitcase Packing List

Tips for Packing Your Carry-on For a Flight

1. Your backpack is an ideal carry-on.
2. Any liquids must be 3.4 ounces or 100 millilitres or smaller per item. If they are bigger (for example, sunscreen), they need to go in your suitcase.
3. Then, your liquids need to go into one plastic bag so it can be inspected by airport security.
4. Pack a reusable water bottle. Once you pass through security, you can fill it with water for the flight.
5. Pack one complete change of clothes into your carry-on in case your suitcase is delayed in France.
6. Include something to entertain you in the airport and on the plane, for example, an activity book and markers, puzzle games, or something to read. Don't forget to pack this book! 😉
7. Add a snack (nothing messy) to enjoy while you wait in the airport.
8. Put a little note in one of the outside pockets, including your first name and the phone number of an adult travelling with you. If you accidentally leave your carry-on behind somewhere, someone can call and arrange to return it to you.

Carry-on Packing List

Time Zones & Jet Lag

It's important to know whether or not France is in a different time zone than your home because travelling to France might cause **jet lag.** Even just a one-hour time zone change can mess you up.

Our bodies know when to eat, sleep, and wake up. But what if all of a sudden, you're in a country where it's five hours later than your body thinks it is? So your body might think it's dinner time, but it's midnight in France! It's way past your bedtime, and you're not tired.

Jet lag can make your trip's first few days difficult until your body adjusts. So what can you do?

A few days before you leave for France, find out what time it is there and begin adjusting your bedtime at home. This way, it won't be such a big shock when you get there.

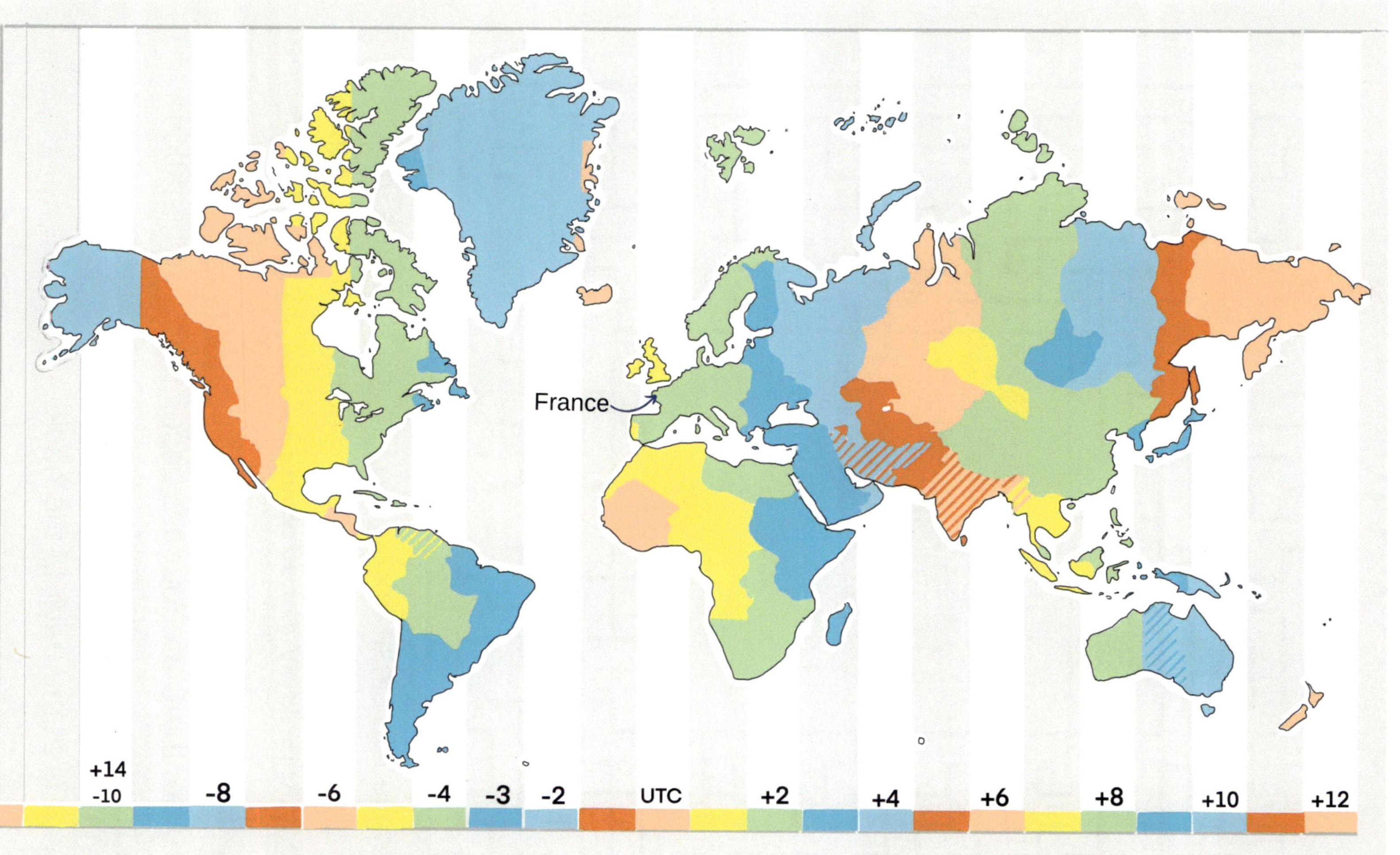

You can use this chart and ask an adult to help you determine the time difference in France

Get to The Train Station

Some people live close enough to France to take a train there. France is also a big country, so even if you had to fly to get there, you're likely to take a train if you visit more than one area.

In this puzzle, there are four entrances to the train station. Can you find the right one?

The answer is at the back of the book.

Airport/Train Station Bingo

Whether you're flying or taking a train, you'll have to wait around a lot. So here's a great chance for a game of bingo!

Just X out everything you see. Can you get a straight line? How about a full card?

A different bingo card is at the back of the book for your return trip from France.

Daily Journal – Travel Day

Date ____________________

Location ________________

Daily Note

The best part of today was:

What I saw today:

Today was exhausting because:

Today I Felt

TODAY'S WEATHER

Today's Transportation

A Picture is Worth a Thousand Words

Draw, write or doodle in this space to represent your day

Daily Journal

Date ____________________

Location ________________

Daily Note

The best part of today was:

What I did today:

I was excited to see:

Today I Felt

TODAY'S WEATHER

Today's Transportation

A Picture is Worth a Thousand Words

Draw, write or doodle in this space to represent your day

Daily Journal

Date ______________________

Location ___________________

Daily Note

The best part of today was:

What I did today:

What made me laugh:

Today I Felt

TODAY'S WEATHER

Today's Transportation

A Picture is Worth a Thousand Words

Draw, write or doodle in this space to represent your day

French Food

France is world-famous for its food. You will be presented with choices you may not have seen at home. To help you prepare, we've created a little cheat sheet below. And to make it even more fun, you can complete the Food Bingo throughout your trip. See how many new and delicious dishes you're willing to try.

Baguette - a long loaf of bread, crispy on the outside, soft on ther inside.
Bisque - a thick creamy soup made with shellfish.
Bouillabaisse - soup made with 4 types of seafood, croutons and garlic.
Cacolac - chocolate milk.
Cassoulet - bean ragout made with duck, pork and sausage.
Chocolate Soufflé - a warm dessert of meringue and chocolate batter.
Confit de Canard - slow-cooked duck.
Coq au vin - chicken stew in red wine and mushrooms (ask for a kid version with a wine substitute).
Crème Brûlée - vanilla custard with a crunchy caramelized sugar top.
Crepes - a thin pancake with fillings that can be sweet or savoury.
Croissant - a pastry made with a lot of butter.
Diablo - lemon soda with syrup. A popular flavour is strawberry.
Escargot - snails with parsley and garlic butter.
French Onion Soup - beef stock, onions, croutons and gruyére cheese.
Macaron - a cookie with meringue, almond flour and buttercream filling.
Orangina - orange juice, sugar and carbonated water.
Pot-au-feu - a hearty soup made with meat and vegetables.
Profiteroles - a cream puff covered in chocolate.
Quiche - a savoury egg custard in a pastry shell.
Ratatouille - a stew of eggplant, zucchini, peppers, onions and tomatoes.
Salade Niçoise - salad made only with seasonal vegetables and olive oil.
Sole Meunière - sautéed breaded sole topped with brown butter.
Steak Frites - steak and french fries.
Steak Tartare - raw ground beef mixed with onions, capers, and pepper.
Tarte Tatin - caramalized apple tart.

Bon Appetit!

French Food Bingo

Are you an adventurous foodie? One of the best things about travel is trying new and sometimes exotic foods. Cross off each item you ate, drank or at least tasted while in France. Can you get a straight line? How about the whole card?

How Did You Score?

no lines = are you a picky eater?

1 line = nice try

2 lines = good job

3 lines - impressive

4 lines = you are a brave soul

full card = you are a foodie extraordinaire!

Daily Journal

Date ____________________

Location ________________

Daily Note

The best part of today was:

What I did today:

Today I tried ________________

for the first time.

It was ______________________.

Today I Felt

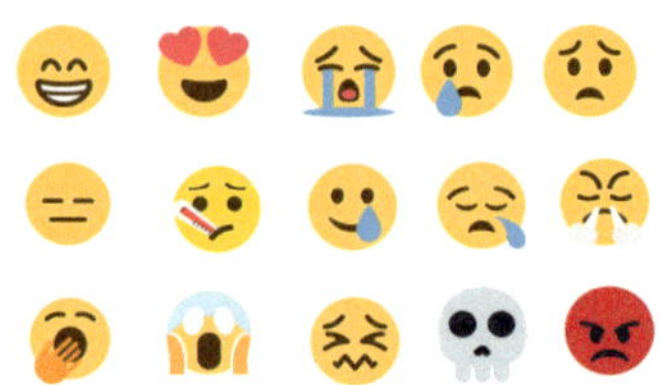

TODAY'S WEATHER

Today's Transportation

A Picture is Worth a Thousand Words

Draw, write or doodle in this space to represent your day

Daily Journal

Date ______________________

Location __________________

Daily Note

The best part of today was:

What we did today:

Where we went:

Today I Felt

TODAY'S WEATHER

Today's Transportation

A Picture is Worth a Thousand Words

Draw, write or doodle in this space to represent your day

Daily Journal

Date ______________________

Location __________________

Daily Note

The best part of today was:

What I did today:

What I ate:

Was it good?

Today I Felt

TODAY'S WEATHER

Today's Transportation

A Picture is Worth a Thousand Words

Draw, write or doodle in this space to represent your day

French Things Sodoku (easy)

draw the correct shape in each square so that each picture appears only once in a column and once in a row.

The solution is at the back of the book.

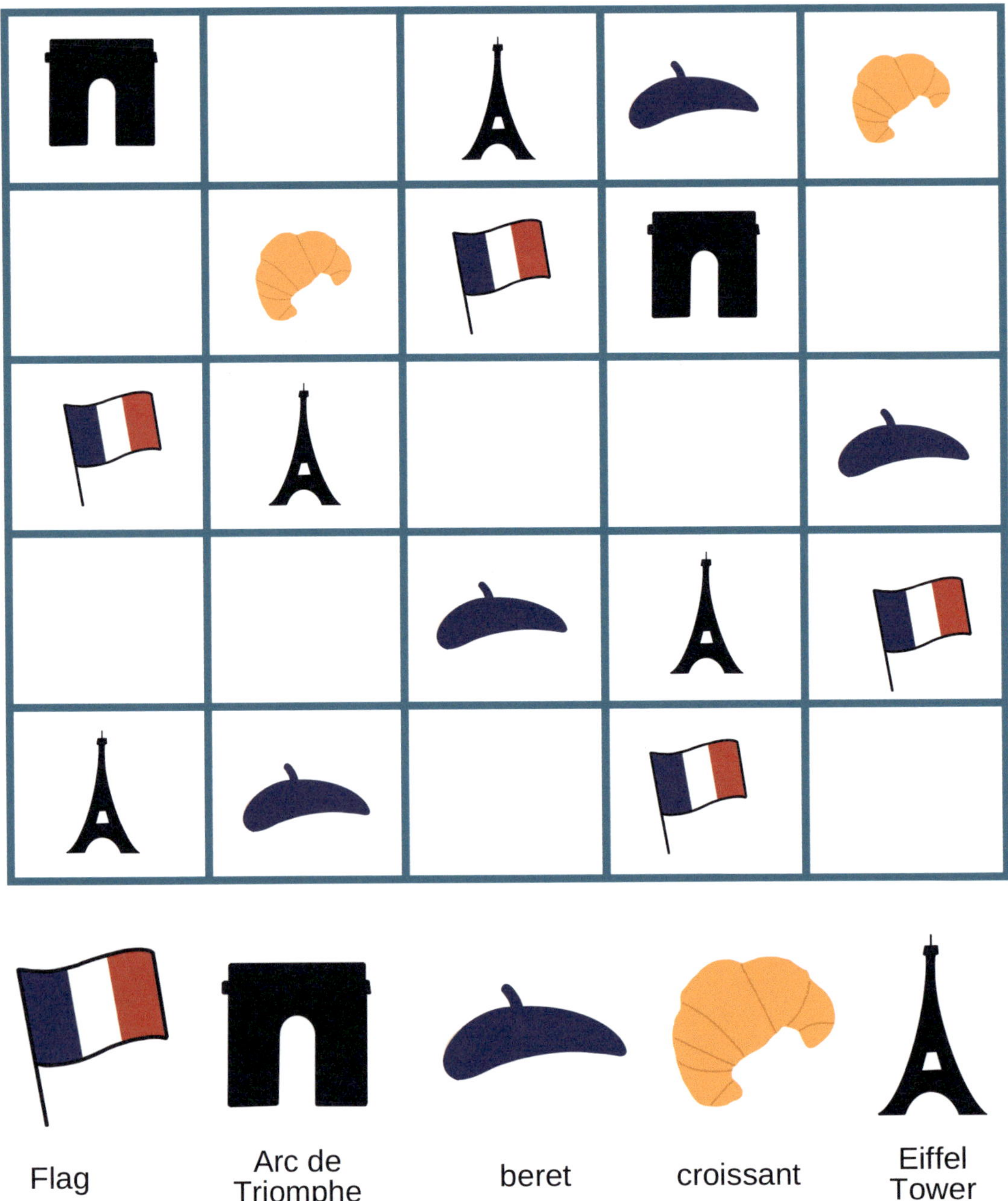

I Spy
CAFE
METRO
4
5
4
6
6
5
7
7
5
6
8
5
6
8
4
7

Daily Journal

Date ____________________

Location ________________

Daily Note

The best part of today was:

What I did today:

Well this was an unexpected surprise:

Today I Felt

TODAY'S WEATHER

Today's Transportation

A Picture is Worth a Thousand Words

Draw, write or doodle in this space to represent your day

Daily Journal

Date ____________________

Location ________________

Daily Note

The best part of today was:

What I did today:

What made today challenging:

Today I Felt

TODAY'S WEATHER

Today's Transportation

A Picture is Worth a Thousand Words

Draw, write or doodle in this space to represent your day

Daily Journal

Date ____________________

Location ________________

Daily Note

The best part of today was:

What I did today:

What made me laugh:

Today I Felt

TODAY'S WEATHER

Today's Transportation

A Picture is Worth a Thousand Words

Draw, write or doodle in this space to represent your day

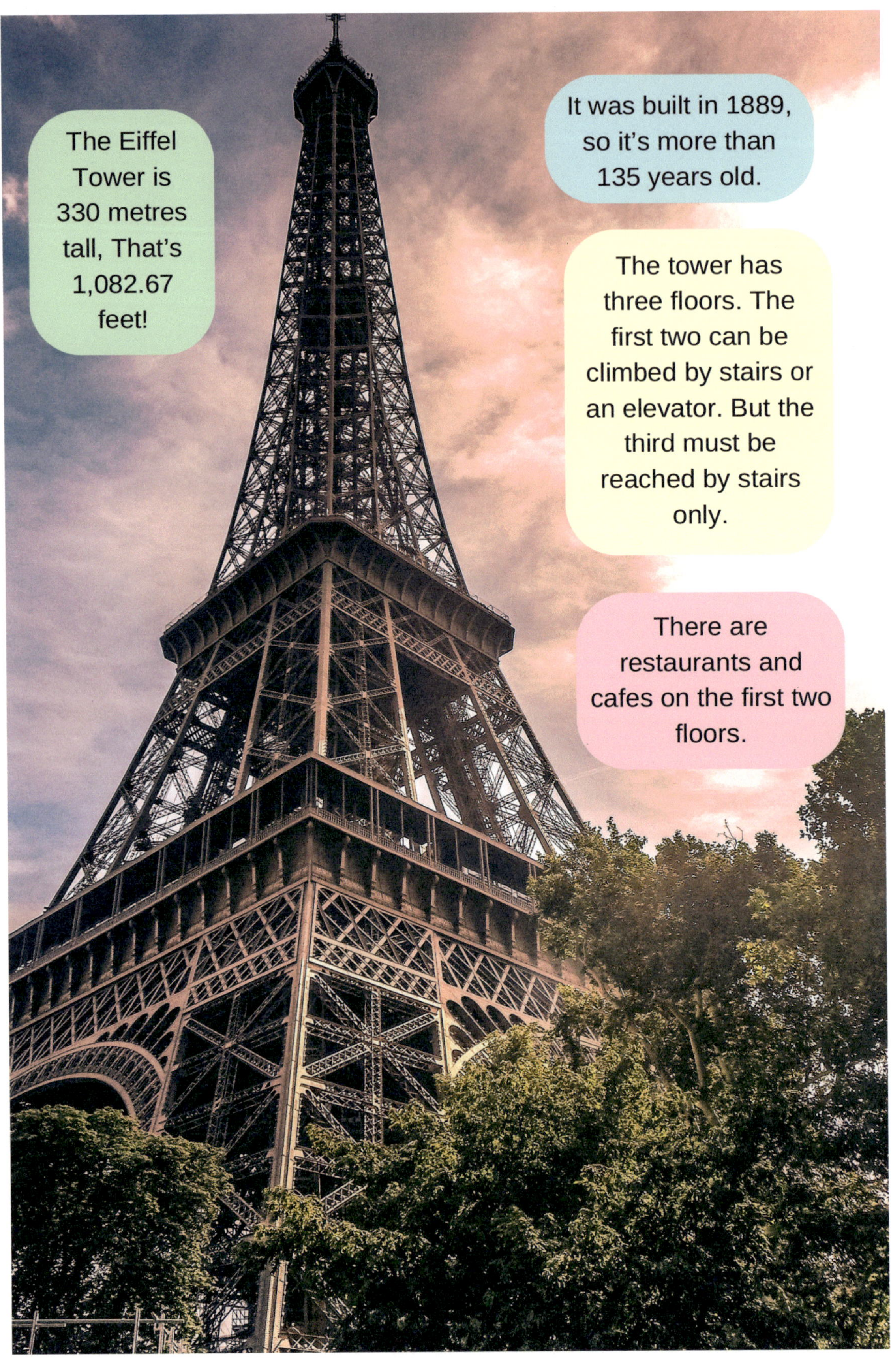
The Eiffel Tower is 330 metres tall, That's 1,082.67 feet!
It was built in 1889, so it's more than 135 years old.
The tower has three floors. The first two can be climbed by stairs or an elevator. But the third must be reached by stairs only.
There are restaurants and cafes on the first two floors.

Find Your Way to the Eiffel Tower

The Eiffel Tower is re-painted every seven years. The colour has always been some shade of brown. BUT... in 2024, in honour of the Olympics, they will paint it gold!

The solution is at the back of the book.

Daily Journal

Date ____________________

Location ________________

Daily Note

The best part of today was:

What I did today:

I was fascinated to learn that:

Today I Felt

TODAY'S WEATHER

Today's Transportation

A Picture is Worth a Thousand Words

Draw, write or doodle in this space to represent your day

Daily Journal

Date ____________________

Location ________________

Daily Note

The best part of today was:

What I did today:

Today I Felt

TODAY'S WEATHER

Today's Transportation

A Picture is Worth a Thousand Words

Draw, write or doodle in this space to represent your day

Daily Journal

Date ____________________

Location ________________

Daily Note

The best part of today was:

What I did today:

Today I Felt

TODAY'S WEATHER

Today's Transportation

A Picture is Worth a Thousand Words

Draw, write or doodle in this space to represent your day

According to the legend of Mont Saint Michel, the archangel Michael came to the Bishop of Avranches in a dream in 708. Michael asked the Bishop in the dream to build a sanctuary in his name. More than 200 years later, the first church was built. Then, a village developed below the church.

Get to Mont Saint Michel Before the Tide Rises

Mont Saint Michel is a tidal island. You can walk across the sand to get there when the tide is low. But when the tide is high, you must take the bridge. Tourists are warned to always take the bridge because the tide rises quickly and can be dangerous.

But just for fun, let's pretend we're walking across the sand. Can you get to Mont Saint Michel before it's too late?

The solution is at the back of the book.

Daily Journal

Date ____________________

Location ________________

Daily Note

The best part of today was:

What I did today:

Today I tried _______________

for the very first time. And it was:

Today I Felt

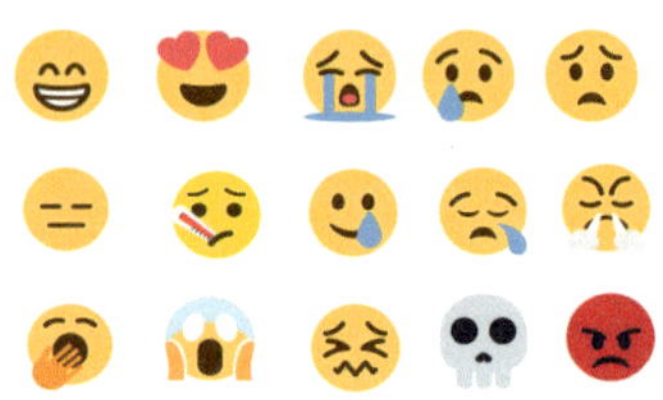

TODAY'S WEATHER

Today's Transportation

A Picture is Worth a Thousand Words

Draw, write or doodle in this space to represent your day

Daily Journal

Date ____________________

Location ________________

Daily Note

The best part of today was:

What I did today:

Today I Felt

TODAY'S WEATHER

Today's Transportation

A Picture is Worth a Thousand Words

Draw, write or doodle in this space to represent your day

Daily Journal

Date ________________________

Location ____________________

Daily Note

The best part of today was:

What I did today:

Today I learned:

Today I Felt

TODAY'S WEATHER

Today's Transportation

A Picture is Worth a Thousand Words

Draw, write or doodle in this space to represent your day

Sample Logic Puzzle

Find out which boy is which age, and what month is each boy's birthday.

	Jake	Joe	Tim	Eric	8	9	10	11
April								
May								
June								
July								
8								
9								
10								
11								

clues

1. Jake was born in July
2. Joe is 11
3. The 9 year old was born in April
4. The person born in May is 8
5. Tim's birthday is in May
6. The person born in July is 10

How to Complete This Sample Puzzle

So, let's take each clue and place check marks where we know the answer. See the grid #1

Next, we'll place an X to eliminate the other options. For example, if we know Joe is 11, we also know he is NOT 8, 9 or 10. And we know that neither Jake, Tim, nor Eric are 11, so we also eliminate those. See grid #2.

Continue by looking at each of the 6 clues until there are 2 checks in each column and two checks in each row.

column ↕ row ↔

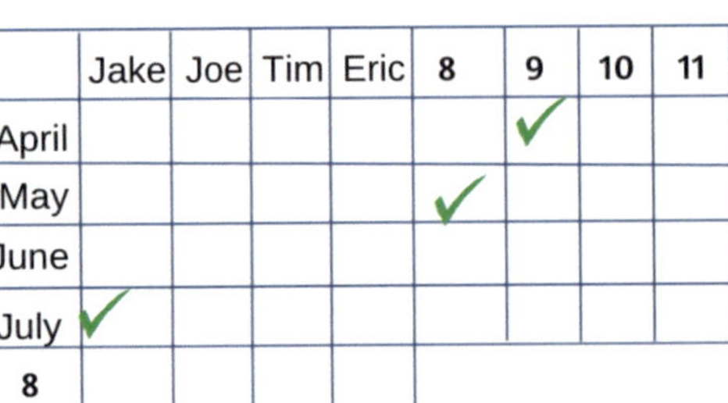

	Jake	Joe	Tim	Eric	8	9	10	11
April						✓		
May					✓			
June								
July	✓							
8								
9								
10								
11		✓						

1

	Jake	Joe	Tim	Eric	8	9	10	11
April						✓		
May					✓			
June								
July	✓							
8		X						
9		X						
10		X						
11	X	✓	X	X				

2

French Vacation – Logic Puzzle (hard)

Four families (Adams, Chong, Garcia, and Jones) vacationed in France. Each family went to either Paris, Nice, Lyon, or Dijon. The vacations lasted 7, 10, 14, or 21 days. Use the clues below to determine where and how long each family vacationed.

	Paris	Nice	Lyon	Dijon	7 days	10 days	14 days	21 days
Adams								
Chong								
Garcia								
Jones								
7 days								
10 days								
14 days								
21 days								

When you know something for sure, place a check in the box. Then place X's in the other boxes for that row and column.

The solution is at the back of the book.

Clues:

1. The Adams were on vacation twice as long as the family who went to Paris.
2. The family that was gone for 21 days visited Nice.
3. The Jones family visited a city with five letters.
4. The Garcia family went to Nice for more than 10 days.
5. The Adams family went to Lyon to buy silk.
6. The Chong family vacationed in the capital of France.

Daily Journal

Date ______________________

Location __________________

Daily Note

The best part of today was:

What I did today:

Today was:

Busy ☐ Chill ☐

Today I Felt

TODAY'S WEATHER

Today's Transportation

A Picture is Worth a Thousand Words

Draw, write or doodle in this space to represent your day

Daily Journal

Date ____________________

Location ________________

Daily Note

The best part of today was:

What I did today:

What surprised me most:

Today I Felt

TODAY'S WEATHER

Today's Transportation

A Picture is Worth a Thousand Words

Draw, write or doodle in this space to represent your day

Daily Journal

Date ______________________

Location __________________

Daily Note

The best part of today was:

What I did today:

Today I got to try:

Today I Felt

TODAY'S WEATHER

Today's Transportation

A Picture is Worth a Thousand Words

Draw, write or doodle in this space to represent your day

French Things Sodoku (medium)

Fill in the squares by drawing the shape to ensure each picture appears only once in a column and once in a row.

The solution is at the back of the book.

French Things Sodoku (hard)

Fill in the squares by drawing the shape to ensure each picture appears only once in a column and once in a row.

The solution is at the back of the book.

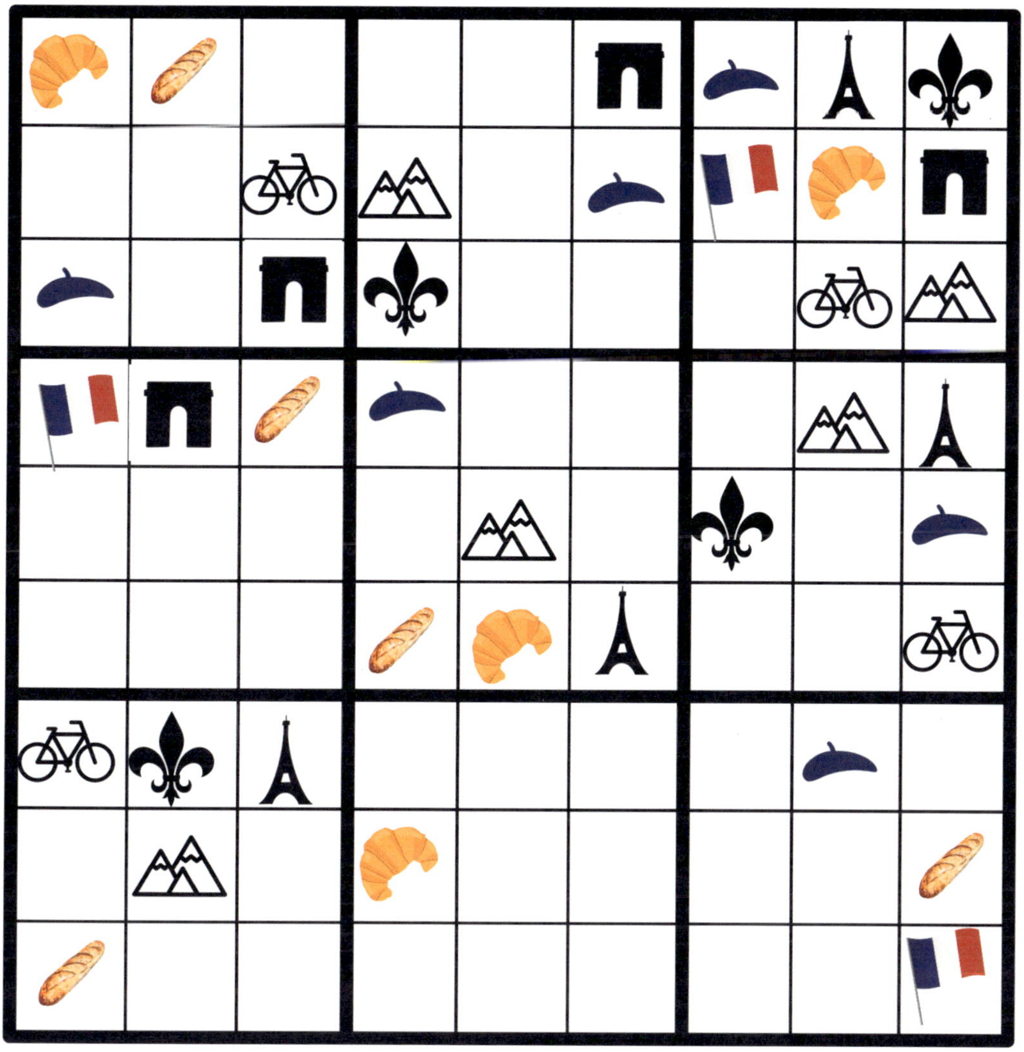

fleur de lys | flag | Eiffel Tower | beret | Arc de Triomphe | croissant | bike | baguette | Mont Blanc

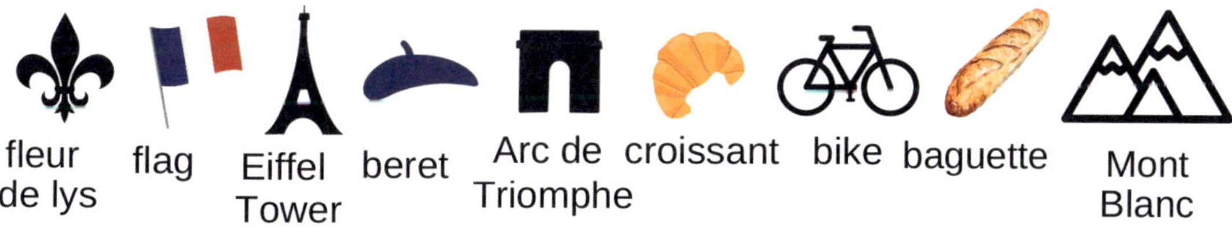

Daily Journal

Date ______________________

Location __________________

Daily Note

The best part of today was:

What I did today:

Today I Felt

TODAY'S WEATHER

Today's Transportation

A Picture is Worth a Thousand Words

Draw, write or doodle in this space to represent your day

Daily Journal

Date ______________________

Location ___________________

Daily Note

The best part of today was:

What I did today:

What made me smile:

Today I Felt

TODAY'S WEATHER

Today's Transportation

A Picture is Worth a Thousand Words

Draw, write or doodle in this space to represent your day

Daily Journal

Date ______________________

Location __________________

Daily Note

The best part of today was:

What I did today:

What I am grateful for today:

Today I Felt

TODAY'S WEATHER

Today's Transportation

A Picture is Worth a Thousand Words

Draw, write or doodle in this space to represent your day

Famous Bridges of France

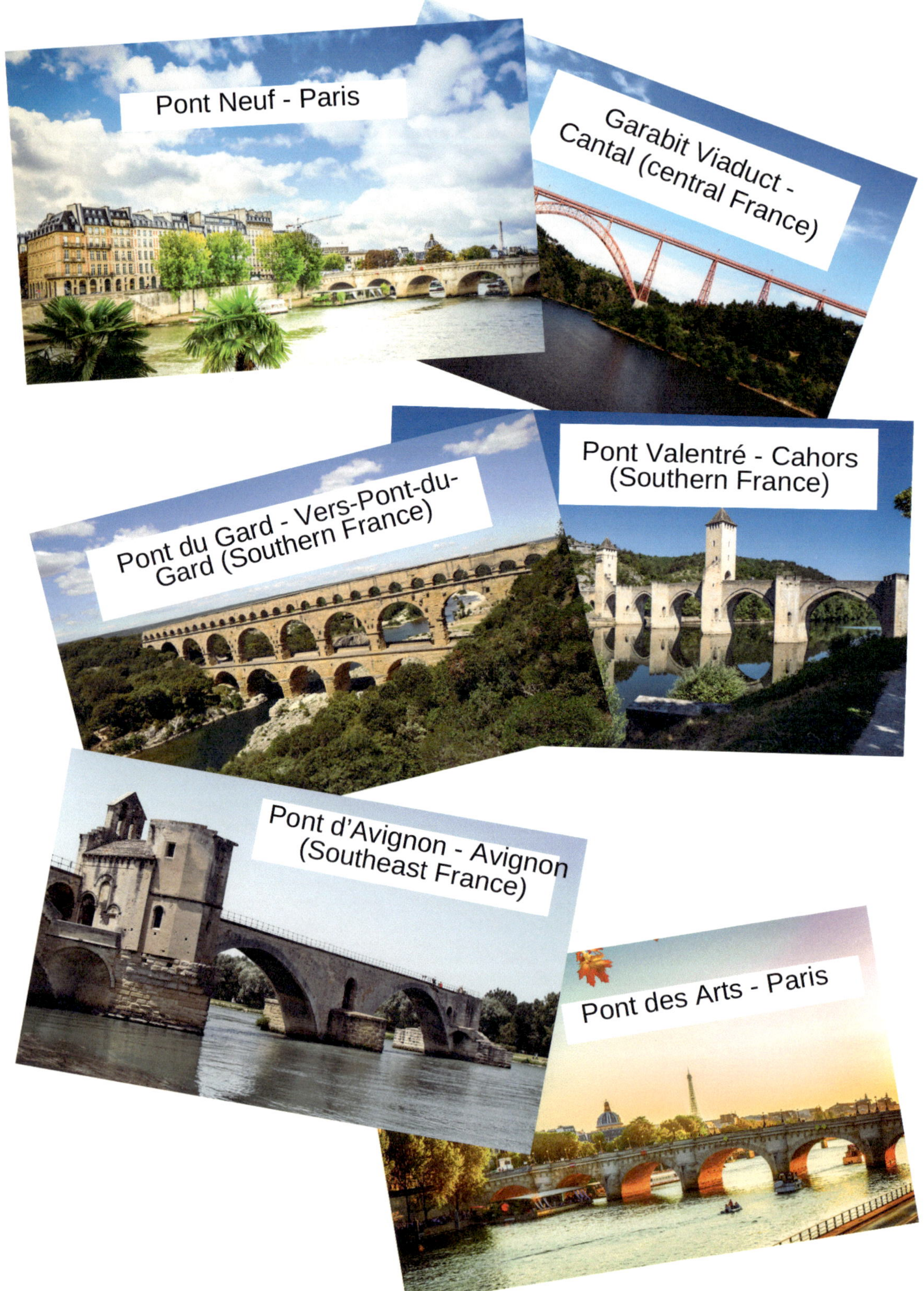

Let's Build Some Bridges

1. Draw bridges (lines) between the islands (numbered circles).
2. The number of bridges connecting must equal the number in the circle.
3. The maximum number of bridges connecting two islands is two.
4. The bridges connect islands horizontally or vertically (not diagonally).
5. The bridges may not cross each other.
6. The bridges and islands must form a single connected group.

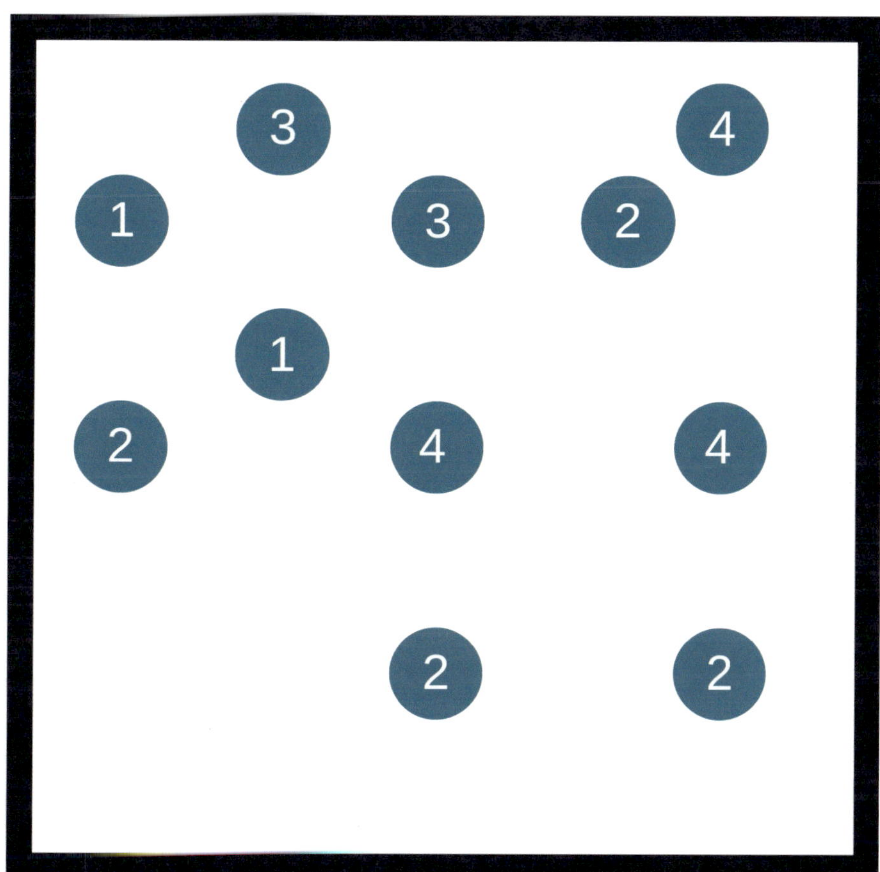

The solution is at the back of the book.

Daily Journal

Date ______________________

Location __________________

Daily Note

The best part of today was:

What I did today:

Who I met today:

Today I Felt

TODAY'S WEATHER

Today's Transportation

A Picture is Worth a Thousand Words

Draw, write or doodle in this space to represent your day

Daily Journal

Date ____________________

Location ________________

Daily Note

The best part of today was:

What I did today:

Where we went today:

Today I Felt

TODAY'S WEATHER

Today's Transportation

A Picture is Worth a Thousand Words

Draw, write or doodle in this space to represent your day

Daily Journal

Date ____________________

Location ________________

Daily Note

The best part of today was:

What I did today:

Today I Felt

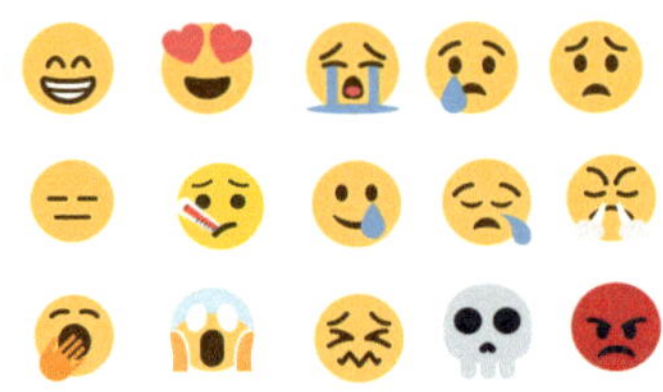

TODAY'S WEATHER

Today's Transportation

A Picture is Worth a Thousand Words

Draw, write or doodle in this space to represent your day

Belphegor the red ghost of the Louvre

According to legend, this ghost has been haunting the Louvre since 1190! Some people claim they can hear him laughing in the halls. People aren't afraid of Belphegor, though. They say he is quite a friendly and funny ghost.

Draw Belphegor

Place a dot for each coordinate pair below (red on the vertical axis, blue on the horizontal). Then, draw the next dot and connect the two. Continue like this until the drawing is complete. The first two set of coordinates are completed for you.

Tip: Don't wait until the end to connect the dots - it's easy to confuse the order.

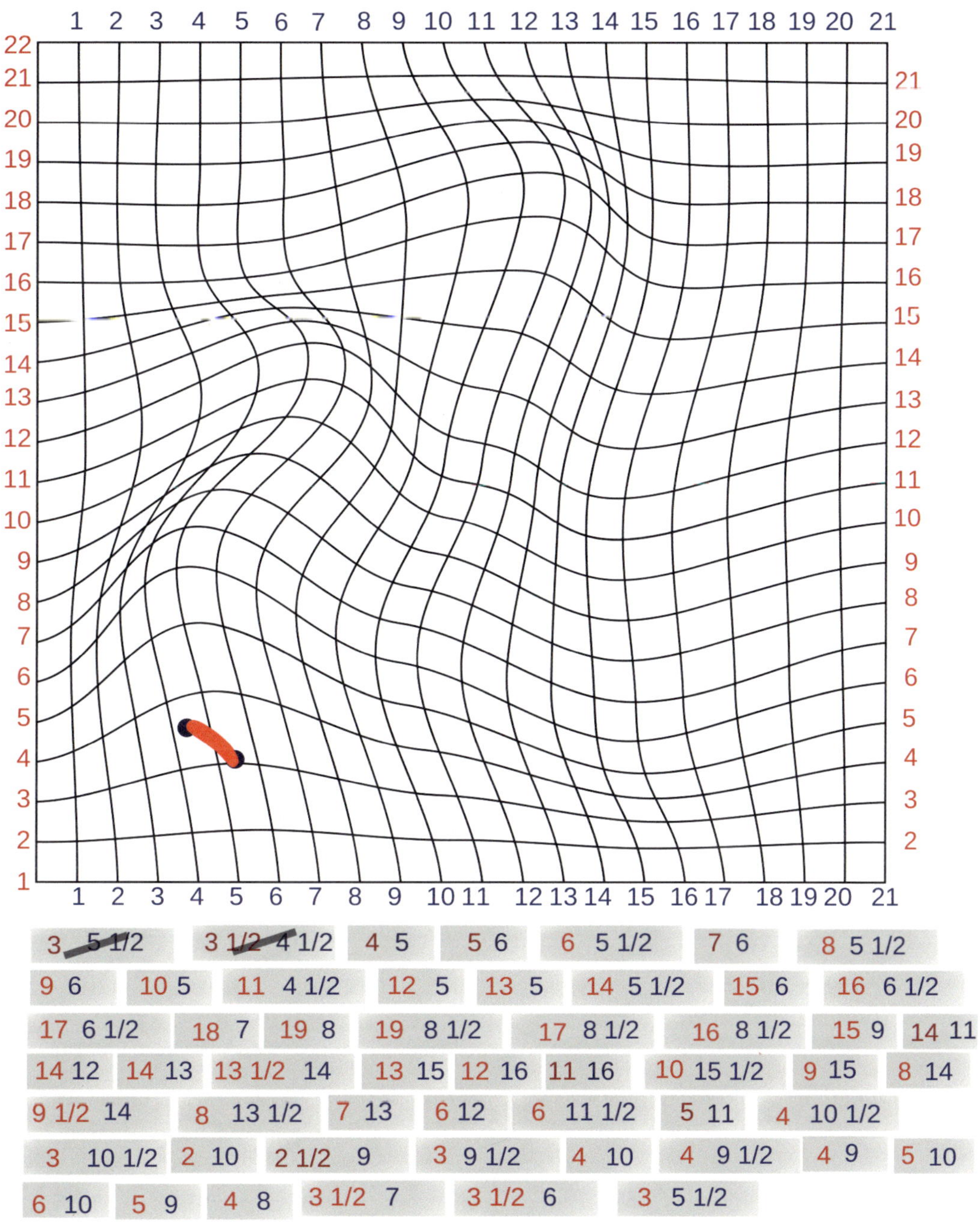

3 5 1/2	3 1/2 4 1/2	4 5	5 6	6 5 1/2	7 6	8 5 1/2		
9 6	10 5	11 4 1/2	12 5	13 5	14 5 1/2	15 6	16 6 1/2	
17 6 1/2	18 7	19 8	19 8 1/2	17 8 1/2	16 8 1/2	15 9	14 11	
14 12	14 13	13 1/2 14	13 15	12 16	11 16	10 15 1/2	9 15	8 14
9 1/2 14	8 13 1/2	7 13	6 12	6 11 1/2	5 11	4 10 1/2		
3 10 1/2	2 10	2 1/2 9	3 9 1/2	4 10	4 9 1/2	4 9	5 10	
6 10	5 9	4 8	3 1/2 7	3 1/2 6	3 5 1/2			

Daily Journal

Date ______________________

Location __________________

Daily Note

The best part of today was:

What I did today:

Today I learned:

Today I Felt

TODAY'S WEATHER

Today's Transportation

A Picture is Worth a Thousand Words

Draw, write or doodle in this space to represent your day

Daily Journal

Date ______________________

Location __________________

Daily Note

The best part of today was:

What I did today:

Today was:

Busy ☐ Chill ☐

Today I Felt

TODAY'S WEATHER

Today's Transportation

A Picture is Worth a Thousand Words

Draw, write or doodle in this space to represent your day

Daily Journal

Date ____________________

Location ________________

Daily Note

The best part of today was:

What I did today:

What made me laugh:

Today I Felt

TODAY'S WEATHER

Today's Transportation

A Picture is Worth a Thousand Words

Draw, write or doodle in this space to represent your day

The Best of France

In My Personal Opinion

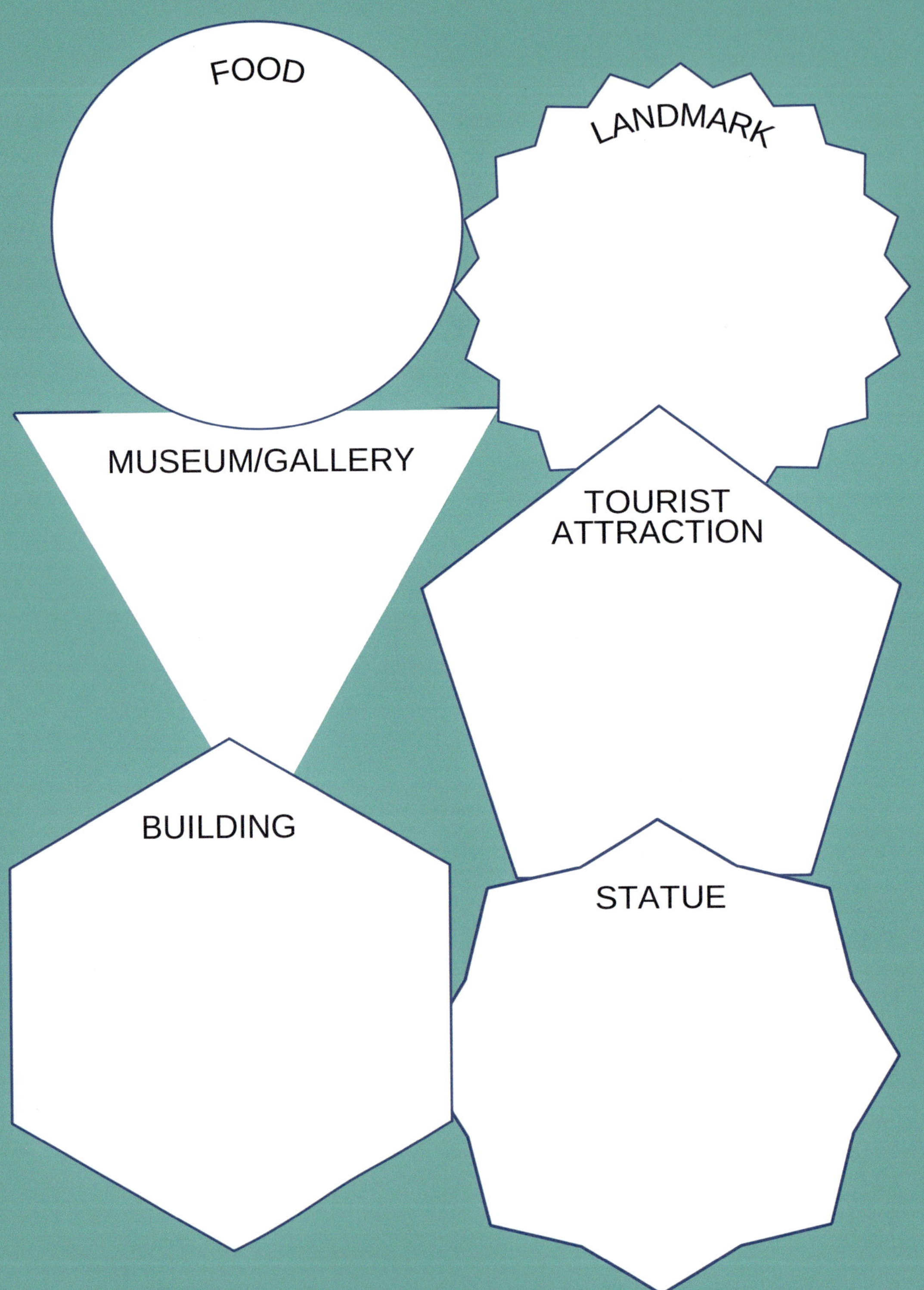

Where I Went

Colour the dots for each city you visited.

Fun Fact: the most visited cities in France are:

1. Paris
2. Nice
3. Lyon
4. Marseille
5. Bordeaux

Daily Journal

Date ____________________

Location ________________

Daily Note

The best part of today was:

What I did today:

Today I Felt

TODAY'S WEATHER

Today's Transportation

A Picture is Worth a Thousand Words

Draw, write or doodle in this space to represent your day

Daily Journal

Date ____________________

Location ________________

Daily Note

The best part of today was:

What I did today:

Who I met today:

Today I Felt

TODAY'S WEATHER

Today's Transportation

A Picture is Worth a Thousand Words

Draw, write or doodle in this space to represent your day

Daily Journal - Heading Home

Date ____________________

Location ________________

Daily Note

Today we leave France and go home:

What I will miss the most about France:

Who I'm excited to see so I can tell them all about my trip!:

Today I Felt

TODAY'S WEATHER

Today's Transportation

A Picture is Worth a Thousand Words

Draw, write or doodle in this space to represent your day

How to Make an Envelope For Your Small Souvenirs

What you'll need:

- scissors
- a glue stick (you can substitute with tape or staples)

Step 1: cut along the dotted lines being careful not to remove the page from the book

Step 2: fold the paper where it says "fold **up**", and make a crease.

Step 3: Unfold from step 2, and lay a thin line of glue where it says "glue".

Step 4: repeat step 2, only this time, run your finger along both sides to glue the paper shut.

Step 5: Once the glue has dried, fold the paper where it says "fold **down**" to make a flap for your envelope.

Now you have a place to keep ticket stubs, tokens, stamps, or any other tiny souvenir you pick up on your trip.

If you prefer, you can also use the pages titled "Souvenirs" to tape or glue small items.

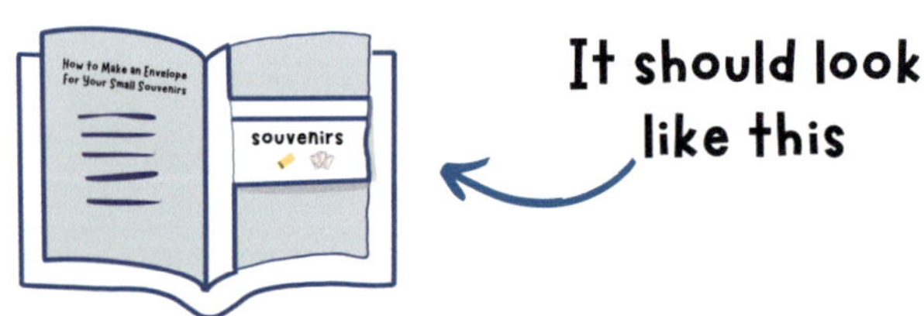

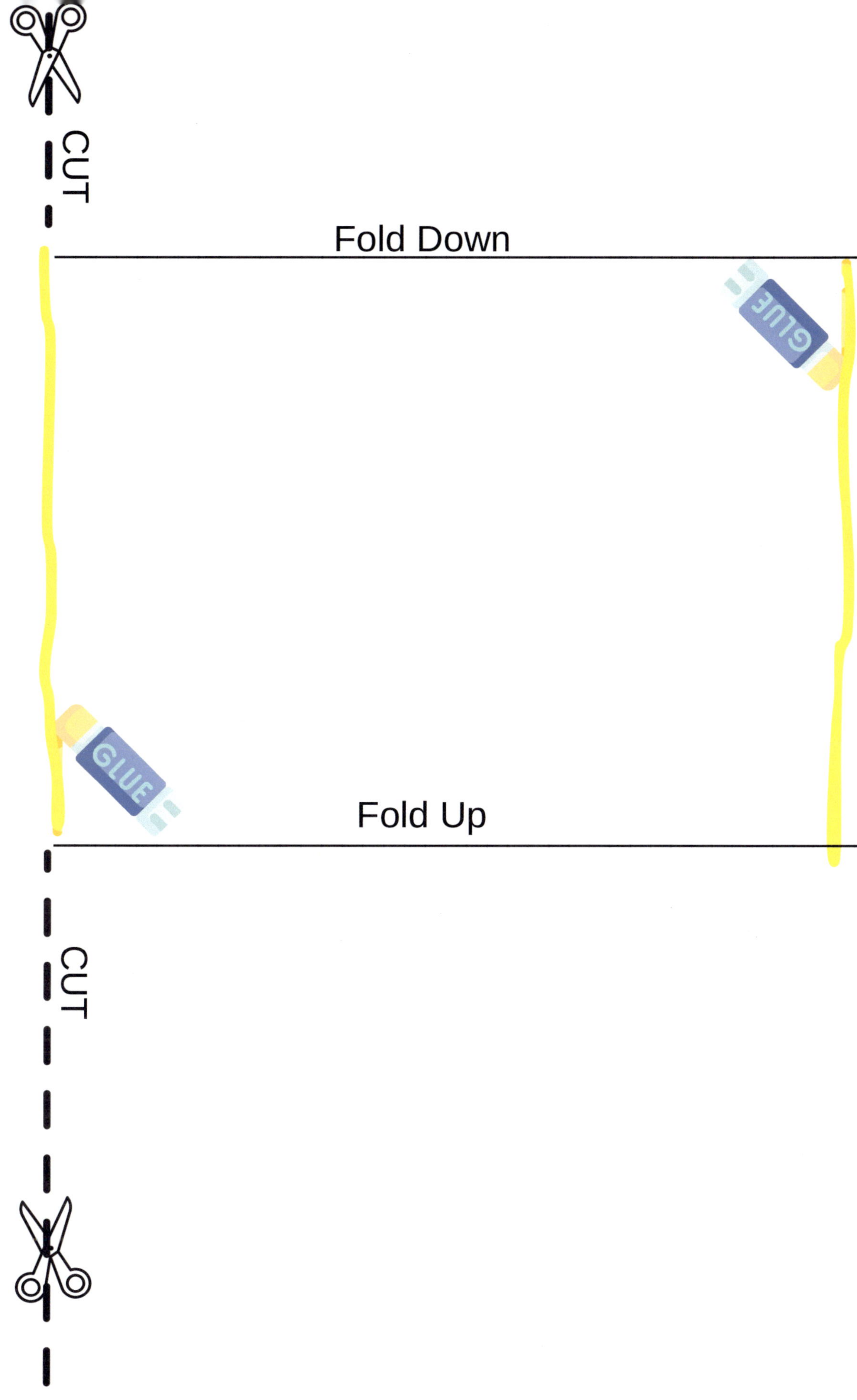
CUT
Fold Down
GLUE
GLUE
Fold Up
CUT

Below is printed upside down on purpose. Once you create an envelope, and fold the paper, this becomes the front of the envelope and right-side-up.

souvenirs

Airport/Train Station Bingo

It's been a great trip to France. But now you must sit at the airport or train station again before going home. Ready for another round of Bingo? Cross off everything you see. Can you get a straight line? How about a full card?

Souvenirs

Tape or glue paper
souvenirs on these two sheets.
Examples of paper souvenirs:

ticket stub
boarding pass
luggage tag
receipt
postcard
book mark
map
menu
program
brochure

Souvenirs

Larger items like a map can be folded first, and then just one section can be attached to the page so you can open it up.

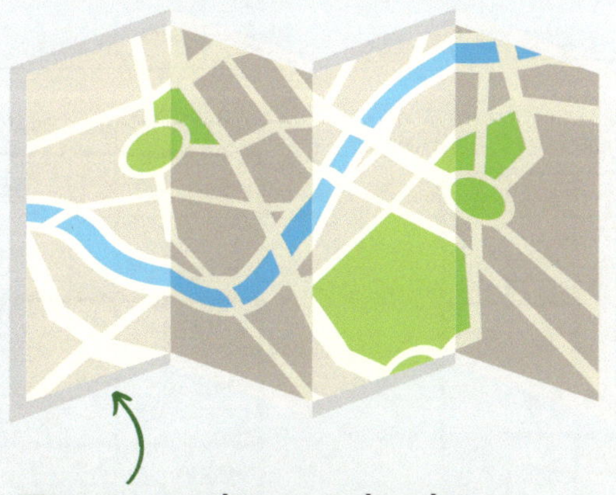

Tape or glue under here then fold it down on top

Answers

Get to The Eiffel Tower

Get to Mont Saint Michel Before the Tide Gets Too High

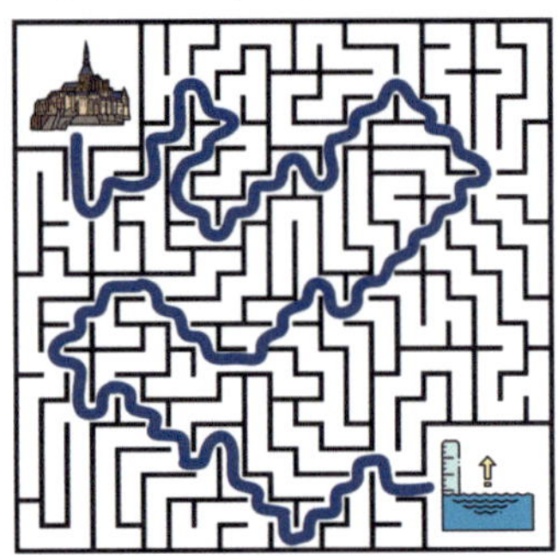

Get to The Airport

French Things Sodoku (easy)

French Things Sodoku (medium)

French Things Sodoku (hard)

Let's Build Some Bridges

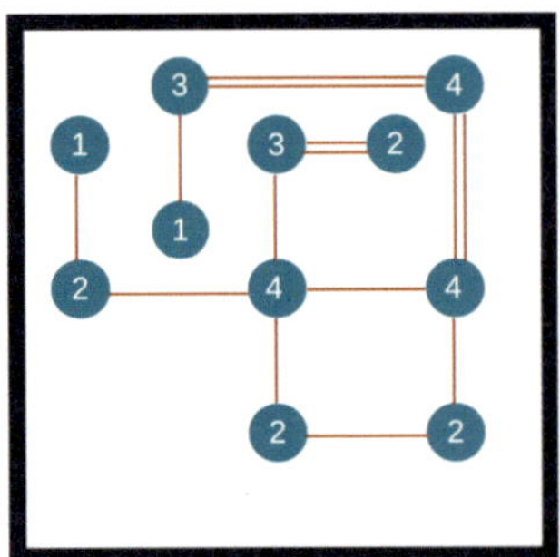

French Vacation – Solution

Four families (Adams, Chong, Garcia and Jones) went on vacation to France. The families went to either Paris, Nice, Lyon or Dijon. The vacations lasted either 7, 10, 14 or 21 days. Use the clues below to figure out where and how long each family vacationed.

	Paris	Nice	Lyon	Dijon	7 days	10 days	14 days	21 days
Adams	X	X	✓	X	X	X	✓	X
Chong	✓	X	X	X	✓	X	X	X
Garcia	X	✓	X	X	X	X	X	✓
Jones	X	X	X	✓	X	✓	X	X
7 days	✓	X	X	X				
10 days	X	X	X	✓				
14 days	X	X	✓	X				
21 days	X	✓	X	X				

Adams went to Lyon for 14 days

Chong went to Paris for 7 days

Garcia went to Nice for 21 days

Jones went to Dijon for 10 days

Clues:

1. The Adams were on vacation twice as long as the family who went to Paris. **Only 14 Is twice as large as any other number. So Adams was gone 14 days and Paris was 7 days.**
2. The family that was gone for 21 days visited Nice.
3. The Jones family visited a city with five letters.
4. The Garcia family went to Nice for more than 10 days.
5. The Adams family went to Lyon to buy silk.
6. The Chong family vacationed in the capital of France. **The capital of France is Paris. So going back to clue 1, we know the Chongs were gone for 7 days.**

We hope you had fun with this book and that it helped you to create a wonderful souvenir of your trip to France.

Made in the USA
Columbia, SC
20 May 2025